# Vignette:

# Glimpses of Mysterious Love

## By

# William and Traci Vanderbush

## 2014

# Introduction

Love.

All have desired it. Some have tasted, touched and seen glimpses of authentic love while wading through the mire of love's counterfeits. Part of its mystery is the way that it makes itself known in the midst of hatred, confusion, and all kinds of darkness. Often, we learn what love is by experiencing what love is not. Many have experienced the outer core of love, but how much of humanity will be able to touch the core of love and be immersed in its fullness?

Being immersed in the fullness of love requires vulnerability, nakedness of the heart and soul, and a life without secrets. I once heard someone say, "You are only as sick as your secrets." And they were right. "Therefore, confess your trespasses to one another, and pray for one another, that you may be healed. The effective, fervent prayer of a righteous man avails much." (James 5:16 NKJV)

Confession to a heart of authentic love brings healing, because the hearer fervently prays for the freedom of one tormented by secrets, and the authentic lover will never treat one according to what they have done wrong, but according to their true identity as a whole person. Once a person has stripped their heart bare, their eyes become opened to see themselves clearly in the mirror, and they are empowered to live a life of wholeness. This is what love does.

The vulnerability and revealing of ourselves that brings the face of love into our vision and takes us into the heart of love, is a risky, sometimes painful journey. But if one pushes past fear and embraces even the difficult parts of the quest, there will be no room for disappointment. Each of our

journeys is different. I have come to
believe that no ones' journey is easy.
Along the pathway created by our
choices and the choices of others,
ultimately we will come to know that
love is not a feeling or philosophy, but
Love is a person. And He has been
with us all along.

In the following pages, my
husband, William, and I share our
thoughts, poetic expressions, short
stories and journal entries about love
and its many powerful facets. We have
kept the format raw, uncut, and
without "professional" refinement,
which is symbolic of love.

Each thought is simply a part of the
unfolding revelation from our own,
personal experiences. We have come
to believe that there is a depth to love
that man can only hope to know while
alive on this earth, and we long to fall
deeper into it, until, of course, we
more fully know Love in Heaven.

We invite you into our thought processes, and pray that you experience the fullness of Love.

~ Traci Vanderbush

Sometimes the purest of hearts are birthed in the darkest places. This is one of the mysteries of grace. This is the mysterious way of love. ~ Traci

# Love is in You

## ~ William

Love.


It is the desire of the nations. The quest of all mankind. The indescribable goal of the human spirit. The gift everyone wants, yet struggles to feel worthy of. To the point where one day a desperation arises within the heart and erupts with a revelation that I absolutely, unconditionally, without reservation or inhibition deserved to be loved because....

And there is where the inevitable pause steals the wind out of the lover's sails, stalls the passion of the heart, and quiets the voice of the spirit with the lying shush of unworthiness. And as long as the quest is for a feeling, a concept, an ideology, a philosophy, the pause has a voice. For love is none of these.

Love is a person. The personification of God, the Word made flesh, the living, breathing lover of our soul, Jesus Christ. He is the origin, the embodiment, the catalyst, the source, authentic Love Himself. And He is so appropriately called in the Scriptures the "Desire of the Nations." So your search then has brought you together; where then is Jesus?

The Bible unveils a great mystery that is Christ within you, the Hope of Glory. It is the revelation of your identity as being in Christ, Who is love, that will continue to unveil the lover's heart within you. He is lacking in nothing, so nothing is lacking within you. And yet His gifts are not given in response to that which you are lacking. He gives because He is good. And so you will give to one another, not because the other is lacking, but because the goodness of Love's gift needs no reason to be given. Love gives because it longs to express itself. And so the longing on the heart of God in creating you was not born of lack, but of love.

You are Love's expression to one another. You are God's expression to this world that is filled with humanity that has become famous for judgment, when we were created to be famous for love. And in loving, we express His workmanship.

The Bible in Eph 2:10 says you are His workmanship. That is the poiema of God, meaning an artistic, created masterpiece. And this I declare over you today: That the poem of God would be recited in your lives. In your words, your gaze, your life. That the poem of Love's heart would be given a voice in this union from this day forward. And that you would make Him, once again, famous for love.

# Familiarity Breeds Love
## ~Traci

Awhile back, as I struggled with a friend's less-than-desirable behavior, I prayed and lamented. This conversation began in my head with God:

"Traci, you must be grace to this person."

"I cannot. It's too much. You do it Yourself, God. You're pretty good at that grace stuff anyway. Besides, haven't You heard that familiarity breeds contempt? Why get close to people?"

"That is not true. In an atmosphere of grace, familiarity breeds love."

That struck me to the core as I was then faced with the decision to come into agreement with Jesus' sacrifice for that person. Would I be a grace-giver? Today, I remind myself of that moment because I need to remember that He once called me 'Courageous Grace.' I want to live up to that name.

# A Death-Defying Act
## ~ Traci

Perhaps our soul is born with a mission. That mission is the death-defying act called "to love." Some believe that man is born without the ability to love and that he must be taught how to love. I disagree. We were all created in love, by love, and for love, no matter what the life circumstances are that surround our beginnings and endings.

Every child longs to do the impossible. At some point in our lives, we dreamed of doing something beyond the ordinary...maybe flying, moving mountains, changing hearts, circumstances, or surroundings. Ultimately, we have longed to defy death. And certainly, love defies death. Love Himself defied death and conquered it eternally.

Since we were in Christ before the foundation of the world, it is in our

DNA to walk deeper into this death-defying act of loving. Letting go of all that prevents us from loving creates an open runway where, upon stepping out in faith, we learn that we have had wings all along.

# The Inception of Image

~ William

So then God created liquid and light and land and life and gave it all color and glued it together with gravity. And man would step out upon the sand and feel the warmth of the sun and the taste of the wind and the sound of the sea and breathe deeply only to say, "Whoa." And man was silent, locked in an inaudible sigh at the knowledge that he was indeed absolutely and eternally loved.

# Journey From Bitterness

## ~ **Traci**

Typically, one finds their passion, mission, or their life message in the very facet of living where their heart, mind and soul were once nearly assassinated by an intensely angry enemy. And sometimes that enemy lunges at our throats through people and things that we consider to be safe. My observations and experiences have led me to a conclusion.

If we carry bitterness and resentment towards someone who has caused us harm, it is as if we are unknowingly feeding and empowering that very spirit that sought our destruction, to take form in such a way that we will not recognize it when it returns to deceive us. Our own bitterness and resentment will cause us to walk ourselves to the threshold of destruction.

When we carry unforgiveness, it is ultimately because of fear, selfishness, and unbelief. For the offended, that statement is offensive. I know, because it once offended me, and it took some time for God to chip away at my hardness and the wall of protection I had placed around my heart. As anger and bitterness slipped away, little by little, my clarity and vision was restored.

Fear, selfishness and unbelief will eventually lead us into the very prison that the assaulting spirit originally attempted to throw us into. Rather than pick up our sniper rifles, we should all surrender ourselves to the fact that Jesus' blood is strong enough to take care of every offense and that He is perfect love that transcends the worst of evils.

As tempting as it can be to retaliate

or seek revenge, I have learned to pray, "Create in me a clean heart. Renew a right spirit within me...that I might not be led to destruction." May we all live in such a way that Jesus gets everything He gave His life for.

As I write this, I nearly tremble with the knowledge that I may someday be challenged, again, by my own advice. Whether my heart feels it or not, I know that this is the right way.

# The Reckless, Raging Fury

## ~Traci

The stunning words of songwriter
Rich Mullins, paint a beautiful picture
of God's grace:

"There's a wideness in God's mercy
I cannot find in my own
And He keeps His fire burning
To melt this heart of stone
Keeps me aching with a yearning
Keeps me glad to have been caught
In the reckless raging fury
That they call the love of God

Now I've seen no band of angels
But I've heard the soldiers' songs
Love hangs over them like a banner
Love within them leads them on
To the battle on the journey
And it's never gonna stop
Ever widening their mercies
And the fury of His love

Oh the love of God
And oh the love of God
The love of God

Joy and sorrow are this ocean
And in their every ebb and flow
Now the Lord a door has opened
That all Hell could never close
Here I'm tested and made worthy
Tossed about but lifted up
In the reckless raging fury
That they call the love of God"

As I encounter people each day and hear their stories, I notice two things. There are the once-defiled who know they have been made clean and whole and there are the clean and whole who do not realize that they are no longer defiled. The experience of grace produces the first...and the experience of judgment creates the latter. It is easy to recognize those who have known the reckless, raging fury known as the love of God.

I marvel at this phrase found in 1 Corinthians 6:9-11: "And that is what some of you WERE." (NIV) "And such WERE some of you." (KJV) Read the following verses:

"Or do you not know that wrongdoers will not inherit the kingdom of God? Do not be deceived: Neither the sexually immoral nor idolaters nor adulterers nor men who have sex with men nor thieves nor the greedy nor drunkards nor slanderers nor swindlers will inherit the kingdom of God. AND THAT IS WHAT SOME OF YOU WERE. BUT you were washed, you were sanctified, you were justified in the name of the Lord Jesus Christ and by the Spirit of our God."

I have met far too many Christians who still do not know just how clean they are, so they continue living a life in which they fall prey to sin, walking in a false identity that they were never created for. They strive to live by the letter of the law rather than by the heart of God. This striving keeps them locked in chains. Christians have often focused on the "will not inherit the Kingdom of God" part and they miss the "were" and the "but" that God so gladly gave His Son for. If Jesus came to set captives and prisoners free, then who are we to keep ourselves and each other locked in chains?

If Jesus could look down from the cross upon the men who beat Him, spit on Him and ripped apart His flesh, and declare these words over them with a heart of compassion: "Father, forgive them, for they know not what they do." ...then who are we to withhold forgiveness? Who are we to call anyone 'unclean' when they have just as much right to the blood that was shed once for all? If someone is unclean, it is up to us to make sure they have an opportunity to know the love and grace that Rich Mullin's describes as a reckless, raging fury.

Grace, furious? You would understand that phrase if you have ever been redeemed from the hand of the enemy.

As for myself, I have gone from being both a prisoner and a captive. A prisoner is one who is held in prison because of something that they did wrong. A captive is held in prison because of something someone else did. I admit that I still have a vigilante side of me that wants the kind of justice that satisfies the bit of my heart that I must purposely and daily give to God. That is why I studied Krav Maga many years ago. There is a certain satisfaction that I once found in hand-to-hand combat, but I learned that unforgiveness and bitterness immobilizes who I really am, and it prevents me from living the life I am meant to live. There are times when I want to "pull out the guns" and then I think for a moment. Would I rather become internally scarred and dead to God's heart, or would I rather lay down in the fields of gold that I have known as 'grace?' I choose the latter.

# Sex

## ~ William

It is not enough to think about love. Love must be experienced, fought for, tasted, rested in. Love's force possesses you, mind and body and when you think of the deepest, most profound way to experience love on a physical level, you think of sex.

I have been a sexual creature all my life, and so have you. If you have grown up in a repressed, conservative household, sex was likely never or rarely talked about. Is it strange that the most thought about subject on the human mind is never talked about, out of a warped definition of embarrassment disguised as respect?

Conservatism tends to live within the confines of this lie that sexuality is a condition that we live with, and we treat it like a disease in our public conversation only to be enjoyed in our private moments. If we are as sick as our secrets, then the church is diseased with the covering up of the fact that even Christians are created to be sexual and to enjoy sex. After all, your genitals did not fall off or shut down when you accepted Jesus did they?

If you grew up in a Christian household, how was it for you as a young person? When you discovered that you enjoyed sexuality, did it feel bad or wrong? For many people, liking sexuality feels as warped to our religious consciousness as enjoying cancer. As shocking as that statement would be, ask yourself this question. Which would be easier to announce to people: that you love sex or that you have cancer? The truth is that for most people they are both equally difficult statements to voice. A cancer announcement would generate sympathy, but a sex announcement would generate looks that display a betrayal of social norms that might look like disgust but it would only be hiding an internally empathetic response from nearly every person in the room. Because the truth is that sexuality is pleasure created by God and deep down inside, everyone knows this.

The purity and beauty of sexuality, like everything else, is defiled by expressions that involve lying and betrayal. William Shakespeare said, "Love all, trust few, wrong no one." To love everyone is the mandate of every person, but our giving of love does not automatically default to sexual expression. How you express love is effective only if it is perceived as love by the receiver, which is why people can have sex and there be no love or even intimacy involved, for within the context of modern human culture, sex is as much a way to experience pleasure as riding a roller coaster, or attending a concert, going to the movies, or getting a foot rub. For many people it simply falls in the category of entertainment.

On one hand, when something so all encompassing as sexuality becomes no big deal, there is a loss of value in its purpose and less fulfillment in its mere existence. In other words, it becomes easy to ignore. For people who struggle with compulsive addictions to all things sexual, this seems like an impossibility. Talk to an adult industry professional however, and you'll realize quickly just how desensitized a person can get. One revelation they do tend to get which is of great value is that there is an intimacy that is found beyond the realm of human sexuality and that is the ultimate quest. For those who believe in it, it is commonly called true love.

The hyper sensitive and ultra suppressive find sex both impossible to talk about casually and ignore casually. In other words, sex freaks some people out and makes their Christian brain short circuit. Like the man who left a church because he stopped in at the gas station across the street and saw a box of condoms for sale. He claimed that it caused him to stumble so much that he could not even concentrate on the message and knew he could never go to a church that was near a gas station that sold such things. That is a true story. When people think that sex is the biggest deal of big deals that has ever been, the struggles with managing appetite and the rational and irrational weaknesses that overtake a person can produce inordinate amounts of shame and guilt. And if there is one thing that is a downer on sexual fulfillment and can kill your buzz quicker than anything it is shame. Secrecy might seem sexy, but shame is most certainly not. Shame will cause people to act out irrational behavior and call it holy.

Shame is religion's way of convincing you that you are evil because of what you have done, where the Holy Spirit is the Father's way of convincing you that you are righteous because of what Jesus has done. See, if I can convince you that you are out of favor with God, it puts you in a position where I can control your behavior by taking responsibility for your life. In the church we call that accountability. And to justify controlling people who seemingly have no self-control, the church has preached some atrocious theology that generates a response motivated by guilt, shame, and fear. And that is where I think Paul's liberating blanket statement of behavior applies so well.

"All things are lawful (permissible), not all things are beneficial (edifying)." Whatever your theological position on God's perspective of human sexuality, even the most liberal of persons for whom anything goes would concede that not everything goes well. Anything that brings shame and pain to the heart and dulls our ability to detect and discern the voice and know the mind of God is of no benefit, and that is what qualifies as sin. For some people, it is an enlightened existence to, rather than change the behavior, simply become convinced that the behavior is fine and should not produce shame and guilt. But ask someone who is hurt or betrayed by your behavior and they would say that such selfish recklessness is no enlightenment to any perspective. No, on this note William Shakespeare had it right. Love all and do wrong to no one.

Love was never meant to betray, to cause pain, or justify lies. Might I offer this suggestion? Share your kindness liberally. Share your commitment carefully. Share your heart rarely. Share your love as liberally as you do your kindness. But give of your sexuality when all four (kindness, commitment, heart, and love) are present in you and presented to you. Ideally defined, a marriage ceremony is supposed to be the public profession that this moment is the convergence of all of these qualities.

The embrace of sexual intimacy is the prized expression of authentic love, and herein is a value and satisfaction far above a selfish, animalistic, physically dominating fulfillment. Genuine intimacy and true pleasure is found in the hand of God who is Love and it is that hand upon your life and behavior that will illuminate the deepest revelation of you as a sexual creation of a very good God.

# Great Sex

## ~ Traci

After more than two decades of standing in line at the grocery store, I have become very familiar with the typical headlines of popular magazines. Some of those headlines read:

Mind Blowing Sex
The Greatest Sex
Deep Sex
78 Ways to Turn Him On
25 Tips From Guys
Be A Sex Genius
The Secret of Sex
Best Sex Tips

On and on the list goes, and I have to wonder, after two decades of reading the same headlines, have they actually figured it out yet? Or are they simply rewriting the same articles over and over, making it appear like new information? The truth is that sex IS amazing and it really does not take a genius to figure that out. It does, however, take a dedicated, right heart to become a spouse who commits to tune in to their spouse, learning what they like, how they feel, and knowing what moves them.

Anyone who claims that it gets dull after being with the same person for many years just is not doing it right, or has become stuck in a routine. (Before I go further, I do want to state that I understand that some people may experience problems due to health or abuses, or other events that have interfered with a healthy sex life. In those cases, I hope those couples will find good counsel, therapy, and/or advice that will lead to a good sex life).

In my opinion, married sex should become better and even, dare I say, more frequent with time. Consider a master musician who values and knows his beloved instrument well.

Perhaps a violin or cello. There is a certain sound that he has become one with, and he knows exactly where to touch and how to touch to create the sound. Each instrument has its unique "feel" and over time, it is as if the two become one. The musician is willing to learn, write and play new songs. If he has become limited to playing the same songs over and over, then he has lost his creativity and passion.

In our early years of ministry, my husband and I often met with couples for their "pre-marital counseling," and one of the first things we would do is have them list their expectations of each other, and we would try to help them be aware of those expectations so that they could meet them. Today, we cringe at the thought! What we should have done is to take the lists and rip them to shreds. The truth is that it is impossible for any human to meet every single expectation of another, and continue doing it for years.

There is something deeper than expectation. There is a mysterious union in covenant that is insanely beautiful and few really learn to see it. Those who dare to walk with another through sickness, difficulties, disappointments, and shakings of all kinds are usually the ones that get to discover deeper facets of union that actually enhance love and intimacy. My questions for those considering marriage are:

Are you willing to walk with this person through their "dark night of the soul?"

Are you willing to lay down your expectations, allowing this person room to grow and become who they are?

Are you willing to pay close attention to, studying and pursuing the heart of the one you love?

What if this person hurts your heart?
Do you love them enough to love them
through it, until they learn to love
more?

   If the answer is "yes," then chances
are that you will get to experience the
amazing, explosive intimacy, power
and blessing of love. And wrapped into
the mix is the package of good sex.
Great sex. Mind blowing sex!

   Now, I wonder again about those
magazine headlines. Have they figured
this out yet?

# The Lover's Job

## ~ William

When God made you, He did so in Love. Everything about who you truly are originated in Love Himself. His Spirit was breathed into the costume you wear with great affection. And it is this Love that defines you, reveals Him, and unveils the boundless horizon of His goodness. You have been designed with a blueprint that originated in the mind of God. You are in the most literal sense, a manifestation of Gods imagination. You are the daydream of Love Himself.

Now you have one job in this life. To be loved. To be loved with outrageous abandon. Heaven has conspired to love you. Eternity has constructed an existence where love shines without inhibition. Do you think that you are supposed to love? That you are supposed to love the best you can in this life? Do you love well? Do you justify loving poorly when you cannot seem to generate enough affection for people? Does the idea of loving seem like work and before you know it the end of the thought leaves you too tired to even begin the effort?

To you, I say you are not doing your job. Remember? Your job is to be loved. God is trying to communicate to you something vital to understanding. It is next to impossible to love beyond the revelation of how loved you are. You cannot generate love for another. Love is a gift that is born of God, and to love apart from that gift is a religious action that is born of a simple desire to please another person. Love, duty, and the fear of man all motivate people to kindness, and the actions are very much the same. But duty and fear will both wear you out, because you are the fuel for their fire, and when you are the fuel, you will burn out.

Love is energizing, invigorating, and supernatural in its ability to infuse you with life and strength in the midst of supernatural effort. Ask God to reveal His love for you and to you, without creating the box of expectation, and position yourself to receive the grace that He has prepared for you from before the foundation of the world. From that place, you will love with far greater effect than you could ever imagine.

# Law Vs. Grace
## ~Traci

Why are we caught by surprise when we ask for the heart of God and we get slammed with trials and circumstances that threaten to pull us away from His heart? Grace is what Jesus is all about, so is it possible to carry the heart of God without being stretched in areas of our lives where grace is necessary?

We will either be shaken by situations in our own lives or situations in the lives of others who we deem as upright, immovable and excellent; challenging us to either grab onto law or cling to grace. It is out of fear of losing control that we grab tightly onto law. It is out of a pure heart, wholly trusting God that we dare to cling to grace. The latter is what love looks like.

Awhile back, I attended a service in

which a particular minister was ministering. A few years prior, he had gone through some personal issues which resulted in the end to a great revival and also a divorce. I see myself as a person of grace, yet I will admit that I was reluctant to be there. Why the reluctance? I suppose it would have been easier for me to accept his re-launching into ministry had he returned to his wife and cut off the relationship that brought a halt to the revival meetings that were taking place. It just doesn't calculate with me that the power of God in His life was not enough to bring healing and reconciliation where it was needed...where covenant would remain unbroken. However...

Here is what happened as I sat in the service: worship time was wonderful and the presence of God, very sweet. "Traci, don't be a spectator here. You are not to judge. All you need to do is be with God and honor

Him," I told myself. I held out my hands in front of me, palms up, ready to receive something from the Lord.

After a couple of minutes, I literally felt a rod being placed in my hands. It looked like a silver rod and it rested across both of my hands. On the left, it said LAW in bold letters and on the right it said GRACE.

I asked God, "What is this?"

Immediately, I got a pain in my right wrist and felt Him say, "Remember the crucifixion." I thought, "Okay, I remember Your sacrifice, Jesus." After I said that, I watched the word 'LAW' fade away until it no longer remained. GRACE remained and overtook the entire rod. "It is My kindness that leads to repentance." His rod is a rod of grace. His correction comes with grace. I see.

Whether this minister is in a right

place or not, it is my responsibility and pleasure to partner with God in releasing the grace that He gave to all of mankind. If we reject someone that He died for, then we are telling Jesus that His blood was not good enough and His grace is not sufficient. If we reject any human, calling them unfit for God, we are telling Jesus that He made a mistake in choosing to die for mankind and we are exalting ourselves as being more worthy than another. Who are we to make such judgments? We have all fallen short of the glory of God and that is why Jesus took us to the cross where we became carriers of His glory.

The revival was a real revival where true repentance, salvations, baptisms, deliverances and miracles took place. Was God blind when He chose to release these things through this man? Did the Lord have a moment where He lacked good judgment when He allowed this man to be on a platform, preaching on His behalf? I think not.

I challenge myself with this question: "If God chooses to pour Himself out through a broken vessel with issues, will I reject drinking from it? Is the darkness of the vessel more powerful than the power of God that comes pouring through it? Can the rivers of living water be tainted by a vessel who is making wrong choices? The answer is NO. Can destruction come because of it? Unfortunately, YES, however, as believers it is our responsibility to steward grace by coming into agreement with Jesus when He was dying on the cross and He spoke, "It is finished."

When the church learns to be graceful as Jesus is graceful, then the destruction will be reversed. The world will not scoff, but will admire the love of the church in lifting up our broken, fallen brothers and sisters. Admit it.

We ALL have broken places and everyone...I mean EVERY ONE is capable of falling. But we have a hope and a Love, and ultimately, we are dead to sin. When we fully comprehend that reality of being dead to sin, we will no longer struggle with a desire to sin, because love will be our motivation, and it will be a natural response to live a pure life.

Ephesians 2:13-16:

13 But now in Christ Jesus you who once were far away have been brought near by the blood of Christ.

14 For he himself is our peace, who has made the two groups one and has destroyed the barrier, the dividing wall of hostility, 15 by setting aside in his flesh the law with its commands and regulations. His purpose was to create in himself one new humanity out of the two, thus making peace, 16 and in one body to reconcile both of them to God through the cross, by which he put to death their hostility.

And in the King James Version:

13 But now in Christ Jesus ye who sometimes were far off are made nigh by the blood of Christ.

14 For he is our peace, who hath made both one, and hath broken down the middle wall of partition between us;

15 Having abolished in his flesh the enmity, even the law of commandments contained in ordinances; for to make in himself of twain one new man, so making peace;

16 And that he might reconcile both unto God in one body by the cross, having slain the enmity thereby

Verse 15 speaks of the law being abolished or set aside. What, then, is the new law? If God is Love and Jesus was His grace expressed upon the earth, and He shed His blood for us, then the new law is Grace. I would call it he Law of Grace or Law of Love.

How ironic that Law ultimately

killed Grace when Grace came to fulfill the Law. And the resurrection of Grace made Grace supreme, wiping out the "rights" of the Law. When Grace was raised up having ALL authority, Jesus breathed on the disciples and imparted to them the power to release Grace to the world (John 20:19-23).

And the Word was made flesh, and dwelt among us, (and we beheld his glory, the glory as of the only begotten of the Father,) full of GRACE and TRUTH...(John 1:14).

Consider this: James 2
12 So speak and so act as those who are to be judged by the law of liberty. 13 For judgment will be merciless to one who has shown no mercy; mercy triumphs over judgment.

The law of liberty frees us from judgment and death if we also impart mercy and liberty to others. Liberty

DOES NOT MEAN taking advantage
of grace. As Scripture says, it would be
foolish to think that way.

Just how free are we? Take in
Romans 6:14: "For sin shall not be
master over you, for you are not under
law but under grace."
Once we get a revelation of that, I
believe our hang-ups will fall off like a
thousand-pound boulder. Sin has no
right to master us. Sin, legally, no
longer has any right to have its hooks
in us.

If we are legalistic, then we
essentially act as if Christ's death was
void of power. Galatians 2:21: "I do
not nullify the grace of God, for if
righteousness comes through the Law,
then Christ died needlessly."
Righteousness cannot come through
the Law. If it were possible for
righteousness to come through law,
then Jesus would have avoided the
most excruciating experience ever.

Law alienates us from Christ: "You have been severed from Christ, you who are seeking to be justified by law; you have fallen from grace." Galatians 5:4

A popularly misquoted scripture is Luke 6:38, where Jesus says, "Give, and it will be given to you. They will pour into your lap a good measure-- pressed down, shaken together, and running over. For by your standard of measure it will be measured to you in return." I say that it is misquoted because I have only ever heard that Scripture being preached on in regards to giving money.

Take note of what Jesus said right before He spoke the words in verse 38. "Do not judge, and you will not be judged; and do not condemn, and you will not be condemned; pardon, and you will be pardoned." Jesus was talking about releasing grace, releasing

pardon and giving up our "right" to
judge or condemn. And when we
release grace, more grace is released
upon ourselves.

When verse 37 mentions "running
over," I think about Psalm 23..."my
cup runneth over. Surely goodness and
MERCY shall follow me all the days
of my life." What a beautiful destiny
He has given to us!

If Jesus is not acting as an accuser,
then who are we to accuse and partner
with the accuser of the brethren,
Satan?

I refuse to be an accuser of the
brethren. I refuse to play judge. As a
Christian trying to maintain a righteous
environment, I played that role for far
too long. I will, instead, agree with
Jesus and accept the good that He
pours out, knowing that the person
who is in the wrong still has a destiny
to be righteous.

If someone continues operating in the wrong and walking in a dishonoring fashion, I have to leave that to God to "fix." If another fall were to happen, it would most likely be due to the fact that our Father is still trying to give us His heart and shake us out of our judgmental state, making His Bride like Him, with a heart full of love, grace, and compassion, for that is when the world will truly be transformed, and that is when revival will be everlasting.

# Dark Nights
## (The Story of a Princess)

~ Traci

She ran and ran, as hard and as fast as her body would go. Fueled by a heart that was exploding with agony and despair, not paying attention to the rocks and obstacles before her, or the people who hiked the path nearby, she ran as fast as she could, her chest heaving as it worked hard to contain the sound of immense pain. Was this world even real? Where was she running to? Who was she running to? She had not thought that far ahead. All she knew is that she had to keep running hard to escape the pain that was crushing her soul and the world that had left its bloodied hooks deep within her heart.

Security and safety was no more. Had it only been an illusion all of these years? Her perfect life story was now forever tainted and stained beyond repair. There was no turning back. That reality left her unsure of everything she was seeing and experiencing. Unsure of every relationship and everything she had ever believed. It seemed as if running was her body's natural response to the spirit within her that was desperate to escape this new reality…this cruel and evil joke of an existence. Perhaps she would run until her heart stopped, and then she would be rescued, saved by death, taken from this realm into a refuge that she could only hope existed.

Her heart trembled at the possibility that perhaps nothing good really existed, even on the other side. Maybe the God that she had long accepted as a loving Father who cherished her as a princess was not even real. Or if He was real, He never loved her to begin with. And perhaps He thought that her desire and belief in goodness and perfection was foolishness. Did He stand by, amused, as her world was ripped apart?

All that was good now seemed like a lie. An endless, evil illusion. Was she part of some divine bet like Job? Just another pawn on the table, being used to prove to God and Satan who was more powerful? What was real? Was love real? Had her Father played a dirty trick on her? The questions came too quickly, one upon another, like a Mt. Everest that made her heart its foundation.

Not knowing how long she had been running or where she was, she suddenly stopped, realizing that no living creature was in sight. There, her legs gave way, letting the weight of her soul pull her to the ground with a crashing force. All was hazy and gray. Color no longer existed. From deep within the core of her being, a guttural cry, a despair-filled wail arose, threatening to rip her chest in two. She was sure that the whole universe had shaken at the sound. There were no words. No form. Just sound that was filled with the ache of abandonment, confusion, and self-hatred.

As darkness fell, she weighed her options of returning home or remaining in the woods to possibly die. Death did not feel like a threat. In fact, it would be a welcomed friend. Yet, responsibilities to those in her life convinced her to pick herself up out of the dirt that had become her closest companion for the last few hours. The mud that formed on her cheeks from being met with her hot tears now seemed like a friendly kiss from the earth, reminding her that she was not alone. The breeze was a more trustworthy companion than anyone she had ever known. Perhaps it was God Himself, telling her that He was, in fact, with her all along. Maybe He was still there. Maybe He was faithful.

As the days passed and her heart was greeted from time to time by the unexpected arrival of hopeless grief, she would run until her soul reached a place of acceptance. Quickly, that acceptance would be met with an onslaught of anger. "How can I accept this?" Running. Running. And running until…

She recalled the night when, while curled up into a fetal position on the floor, soaking in a lake of tears, she had felt the arms of an unseen Father. As she noticed the presence, her weeping halted. Warmth came around her body and she felt herself being rocked like a baby. Back and forth. Gently. Silently. Tears once again filled her eyes as she sensed the whisper of Father God in her ear, "I am so sorry. I am so sorry, my princess. I am right here. I promise that everything will be all right. I love you."

As she remembered that night, she realized that she never had need to run again. As any princess would do, she

became aware of the golden sunlight
that seemed to reveal the glistening of
diamonds on the road, so she lay
down, in the street, hugging the ground
that glistened with love. It was an
obvious path to paradise, restoration
and renewal. As she lifted her head,
the world seemed to light up with
brilliant color. Everything was reborn
and alive, brimming with hope,
promise and the supernatural power of
forgiveness. No matter what her
battered heart would try to tell her, she
chose hope. She chose life. Once
again, she chose love. And love would
always remain.

# You are Most Loved When You are Most Known

## ~ William

Every relationship is an opportunity to be a character in a play, and for those who have control issues, they take the director's chair. Maybe not with conscious intent, but they just cannot help but predict the next series of events, sentences, words. If you are the director type, you probably do not even realize that there are people out there who do not think the way you do. Or maybe it is because you know there are people who will not take charge that you start calling the shots.

Relational directors have a hard time with the cast members who will not cooperate. The lines are annoying, the blocking is all wrong, and the whole plot line of the relationship gets thrown off. Strip all of this control away and bring it down to simply absorbing and processing the story of another. If you are invited into it, then offer what you may. But the question is, can you love a character that you cannot direct? Can you embrace a person you did not create? On the other side, we will call this person the supporting player. They look to the directors to find out who they are supposed to be, but by themselves they may be something totally different. They are not weaker, and may even look down on someone's need to control and simply go along with it like an adult condescends to a child's imagination to sip tea out of empty miniature teacups and be called a different name altogether.

Giving in does not hurt and, in fact, makes the relationship amusing. In their own way, the director and the supporting player work with each other to produce their relational story. When it stops working, the story ends. Authentic love lets another person's character develop unhindered and fully accepted. It finds the fascination in the organic spirit and sees the beauty in the scarred soul. It can see you at your brightest moment of heroism and your darkest moment of vulnerability and loves you still.

When you are seen for who you are, and accepted anyway, that is love's expression. If you cannot be known, you will not be loved. Love may be given, but to your character, not to you, and it will always remain just out of your heart's reach. True love is magnified by honesty and acceptance. Magnified beyond words. True love will leave you speechless, breathless, wide eyed in wonder at the tenderness with which it embraces your overworked heart and leaves it at peace.

There are no walls in love's theater. True love gives up the right to yell, "Cut!!" and allows the cameras to keep rolling, even when the script is not perfect, even when the props are not in place, even when the budget is not there, when the reviews are lousy, when the love scenes are awkward, when the music is wrong, when the lighting is off, when the cues and timing are poor, none of it matters. Love always sees a masterpiece.

# Love Makes You Strong, Loving Makes You Brave

## ~ William

There is no weakness that cannot be erased by being loved. It is the ultimate force of empowerment and motivated by the knowledge that you are loved. There is literally nothing that seems impossible. Consequently when you return that love, fear completely evaporates under its molten intensity. It is a relational cycle of superhuman acceleration that sees a mountainous obstacle to be as unthreatening as a house of cards and shakes the earth beneath your every step as if the entire universe is in awe at the spectacle of your fearless courage.

I have wondered at 1 John 4:7-8:

"Beloved, let us love one another. For love is of God and everyone that loves is born of God and knows God. He that does not love, does not know

God, for God is love."

I believe the key to every good and perfect thing in this life and eternity is hidden behind the revelation of how loved we are by Love Himself. To the extent that you realize you are loved, you are empowered to love, equipped with strength, and in loving you are filled with the courage of heaven. We are designed to be an expression of the Love of the father to one another. It is as if God is embracing one person through another.

No doubt God loves in and of Himself apart from us, but He is not apart from us. And that understanding of union equips us to love beyond what we thought we were ever capable of but inwardly wished we were. And you are. Your ability to Love is not tied to your personality, your training, your upbringing, your past, or your present. Your Love is in surrender to the Holy Spirit of God to simply do what He does through you.

"Fallen From Grace"

~Traci


I have often heard Christians and non-Christians alike, both refer to someone as having "fallen from grace" when they committed a sin. All of my life, I believed that term was being used correctly, until I thought about how it made grace seem so fragile and powerless. How could Jesus go through such hell and sacrifice, only to lose someone to a moment of weakness or stupidity?


"He fell from grace." Does that statement hold any hope? Is it a done deal? A fall from grace? The end?


As I fell asleep one night, pondering this statement, I heard these words ringing in my spirit: "People do not fall from grace. They fall INTO grace." I drifted into a dream in which I saw shamed people being shoved away by the church, pushed over a cliff. At the bottom of the cliff stood Jesus, and He was catching them and embracing them with an embrace that caused scales to fall from their eyes. They could see clearly, and when they saw Jesus, they embraced Him.

The next day, I decided to look for the scripture that mentions falling from grace. I was surprised by what I found.

Galatians 5:4: "You have become estranged from Christ, you who attempt to be justified by law; you have fallen from grace." (NKJV)

"You who are trying to be justified by the law have been alienated from Christ; you have fallen away from grace." (NIV)

Wow! "Fallen from grace" is actually when a person denies the gift of grace and they try to justify themselves by gaining righteousness through their own acts. This verse has nothing to do with someone falling into what we typically think of as being sin. Self-righteousness and our own personal disciplines do not contain the power to bring us closer to Christ, or to walk in union with Him. According to Scripture, self-righteousness only alienates us from Christ.

May we never fall from grace.

## If Momma's Not Happy...

~ William

I have found that one of the
vulnerabilities of loving is that you
have just sutured the artery through
which your happiness flows into
another person and now you both
contribute to the collective happiness
of one another to fullness of life, or cut
it off to the depression of both. Either
way, you have just become Siamese
twins joined at the heart, and though
you may retain individual interests and
personalities, when one is not happy,
the other is not either. I do not think
this is a design flaw or a problem. I
believe this is a testimony to our union
with God and one another.

When I do not believe God is
happy, I reflect that condition toward
this world. We reflect the perceived
mood of the object of our affection. If I
look at my wife and she is looking at
something with an angry look, without

even realizing it, I mirror the same look in the same direction. As if I am displaying my distaste for whatever is causing her normally beautiful smile to scowl.

We display our love and demonstrate our union for another by taking their mood or the emotional overflow of the condition of the heart, and exaggerating it, just to make sure they know that we empathize. If they are sitting there happy, we get up and dance. If they are angry, we look for someone to fight. We mirror them and raise the stakes. How does someone else affect you like that? Because you are joined in heart.

Sometimes love will see the heart of the lover going to a place that will cause damage, and in that moment, love is demonstrated in conflict. That is, someone you love disagrees with you. Disagreement is not always a lack of love. Sometimes it is an act of love. And someone who loves you and is not in agreement with you is not your enemy. As a matter of fact, they may save your life, for in standing against your will to self-destruct, they are actually saving themselves too. Let them. After all, you are sharing one heart.

# God Moves Despite Doubt
## ~Traci

I have spent many quiet moments running, walking, dancing and visiting with God at a certain grove of trees. I would often stop in that place, removing my headphones, which carried the sounds of worship by Misty Edwards and Kristene Mueller-DiMarco, and I would lean into the atmosphere hoping to capture an audible sound coming from the mouth of God. I hoped to experience a physical brush with an angel's wing. I knew they were there. I could feel them.

Why would I come to this spot? I had been battling something that I never experienced before with God. I felt a tinge of doubt and began to question His ways and His motives. I will admit that there were moments when it was more than just a 'tinge' of doubt, but my spirit would not let me stay in the talons of unbelief for long. It is quite frightening what happens inside of a person when unbelief finds a moment of agreement within. Death comes. The death of hope. "Christ in me...the hope of glory," I would often repeat to myself. "God, I need you to show up. I have seen Your works before and You have taken me to amazing places, but I need You to come to me right now."

I would sit, staring into the grove of trees that was surrounded by thorny bushes, poison ivy, and rocky ground that most likely hid the entrance of a snake's den. I saw beauty in these trees and there was one in particular that I longed to climb. I envisioned a wooden swing hanging from its massive arm that stretched over what looked like a magical place that existed only in my childhood imaginations.

I noticed a clearing between two

trees and I imagined a cabin there...a refuge for me and my husband...a cozy place where we could dream and write. A place to just...Be. I was urged to walk into the clearing but did not for fear of stepping on a snake or poison ivy. I shrunk back from the hopeful notion of finding something special there and walked back home while revisiting my doubts. "If only I could clear that section of land and enjoy being there."

For more than three months, day after day, the same scenario. Until... Finally one day, as I was dancing and swirling around in circles past this same grove of trees, I noticed that the land had been cleared!! The grove was clear and the large oak with the imaginary swing held its massive branch out, as if inviting me to explore. I slowly stepped towards the tree, inching closer, relaxing as the joy of discovery came over me. "New ground! New territory! What I hoped to see is now uncovered."

I sensed God's presence strongly and deep inside of me I heard this: "Even in the midst of your struggle with doubt and unbelief, I was working on your behalf. The path has been cleared. You are free to step into the wide, open spaces where the enemy cannot go and you will see your dreams become a reality. All of this, I have done for you even though you did not see it. This is My grace." A smile came across my face. Joy bubbled up inside of me. I ran home, eager to share with my husband.

This is the grace of God...that He gives what we do not deserve and He takes away the punishment that we do deserve. I never believed He would do it, but even in the midst of doubt, God moves.

# Things Worth Knowing

## ~ William

If schools wanted to teach some things genuinely worth knowing, they would teach you how to be famous. They would teach you how to be rich or how to be poor. They would teach you how to understand the mind of someone else. They would teach you what to say to someone who is dying. They would teach you how to love well and be loved well. Giving and receiving love; now there is a big one to learn.

Though everyone both gives and receives, people sway to emphasize a lifestyle of one over the other. And you can see it in the eyes. Why the eyes? When you have something to give, your eyes show it, and when you have something you need, your eyes reveal it. When a giver and a receiver lock eyes, there is an unspoken demand that is initiated. Receivers do not often lock eyes with each other because they cannot see past themselves. Givers do not often lock eyes with each other because they have difficulty receiving. This is probably why opposites end up attracting and also why marriage therapy is a huge business.

It is not very often that you find two givers and two receivers falling in love, but they should. When you see that you have what another lacks, you find what appears to be a fit. But it only exists in the context of recognizing the lack in someone else and pretty soon their weakness and lack of appreciation for what you have produces conflict, where all of the books tell you ought to be a complimentary fit.

Opposites do attract, to the inherent need to fix each other. The truth is we fix ourselves in the very exchange of love. As long as love is passed back and forth there is relationship and as long as there is union there is life. For if the one you love and the one who loves you happen to be the same person, you are in a most rare and fortunate position. These are things worth knowing in life.

# Climbing the Mountain of Grace
## ~ Traci

I have been climbing a mountain called Grace. Many times, I became weary of giving grace, trust and love because it often resulted in another painful experience. I would find myself in a good, seemingly safe place on the side of the mountain, but the pinnacle seemed out of reach. Disappointment and pain, betrayal and disillusionment would come and I would find myself spiraling down into a deep pit of insecurity, anger and sadness.

Why did joy seem to escape me? Joy and grace were like the precious jewels that were locked away behind numerous locks and barriers. I could capture glimpses of its brilliant light, but I could not touch or feel it.

I became weary of the climb, but more importantly, I became weary of the pit. Would I press through and reach the pinnacle of grace? Did I actually have it within me to continue loving, forgiving and believing the best about His Bride? Would I let my fears and insecurities keep me from peering over the mountaintop, frightened of what may be on the other side?

When I finally gave my pain, doubts, and fears to God and asked for His heart and thoughts, I became saturated with His presence. I no longer asked Him to come into my heart. Instead, I asked that He take me into His heart. I found unbelievable, indescribable joy. I made it to the peak and the view is magnificent, yet I know there is more. There is a depth to grace that may take a lifetime to discover. The little bit that I have already experienced convinces me that God's love is real and penetrating. I dare you to make the climb.

And we have known and believed the love that God has for us. God is love, and he who abides in love abides in God, and God in him.
1 John 4:16


There is no fear in love; but perfect love casts out fear, because fear involves torment. But he who fears has not been made perfect in love.
1 John 4:18

# The Comprehension of a Promise

~ William

When I was younger I made flippant promises. They were not promises that I intended to break, nor were they promises I did not care about. Rather, I like a challenge. A promise was a self-imposed assignment that, if completed well, would result in the happiness of another and the increase of reputation. So I challenged myself with the phrase, "I promise...". Far more daunting was the wishful command in the form of a question, "Do you promise?" Either way, it was a game to be won, unless it is lost, then it is no longer a game.

I was married at the age of 18, which puts our now two-decade marriage in a rare bracket of those who have made it this far having started so young. We were young enough to have undergone quite a few personality changes over the years and through the evolution of likes and dislikes, I have learned something quite valuable. I learned that it is possible to fall in love with the same person more than once in a lifetime. If you are unwilling to do that, then one day when they wake up and are not the person you married, you will find a way to justify breaking the promise.

Promises are not meant to be the bars that imprison us within the confines of a miserable existence of our own construction. They are made in moments when we realize that this thing that is being promised about is very important. A promise says that this important moment needs to be remembered. Promises are reminders that, at one time or another, this thing promised was important enough to warrant the use of the word in the first place. When you forget that it is important, you can still remember your promise. And rather than be angry at the promise, maybe take a minute to remember the moment in which the promise was made, and know once again why it was so important.

If that which was important then is still important now, keep the promise and rejoice at the reality that there was something in your life important enough to call for a promise to be made in the first place. Those moments are a gift worth treasuring.

# The Power of Covenant
## ~ Traci

Why would someone of royal status desire to exchange their clothing with a poor shepherd and commit their life, loyalty, and support to them?

In studying covenant, one story that I referred to was the relationship between David and Jonathan. This is a true story that some have tried to twist in an attempt to support their agenda, however, I would like to focus on a fact that few seem to acknowledge.

The beauty of the story is this: When Jonathan, the son of a king, saw how a mere shepherd boy conquered a giant that everyone feared, Jonathan was intrigued and drawn to the anointing of God that rested upon David. He saw the favor of God upon David and recognized what he carried, and I believe that is what drew Jonathan to desire a covenant relationship with this young man.

In 1 Samuel 18, Jonathan gave his own robe to David, along with his sword, bow and his belt. Imagine a warrior prince giving these valued possessions, giving his identity to a shepherd boy. That is exactly what Jesus did for us when He allowed man to draw out His blood and rip apart His flesh. He was making covenant with us, stripping Himself of His robe of righteousness and taking upon Himself our shame...clothing us in His righteousness and making us priests and kings, a royal priesthood.

The belt represents strength. Jesus traded us His strength for our weakness. He gave us His sword, His weapons, in essence, taking upon Himself our own enemies. And in turn, anything that is an enemy to Him is an enemy to us. We are in covenant. And through grace, and His invitation to man to be in union with Him, He has imparted the ability to turn adversaries into advocates.

Why would a King be drawn to make covenant with people like us? He sees what we carry...the seed that He placed within us. He breathed life into us and predestined us to be carriers of His glory. To allow us to remain apart from Him and live a life less than what He created it for is against His nature. That is why He came.

The most amazing part is that He keeps His covenant with us. Humans have extremely high expectations when it comes to promises, but God has been merciful to us beyond what we deserve, as He continually forgives when we fail to meet His "expectations." He does have great expectations FOR us, and He is patient enough and loving enough to forgive us and love us back into our destiny.

Covenant is stronger than we realize. The power of the blood of Jesus lies far beyond our ability to comprehend. Ask Him about His covenant with you and let Him reveal how you have been clothed in His righteousness, prepared for battle and wrapped in His arms that never give up on you. Your life may not be perfect, but it can become more beautiful than you have ever imagined.

## They Are Not the Answer

### ~ William

We live with questions. Lots of them. And to fall in love is often to find someone who is the answer to our questions.

Who am I supposed to be with?

Who will love me?

And we ask them questions that we ask about ourselves.

Why do you love me?

What about me is there to love?

What made you love me in the first place?

They are all the same question really, just in different versions.

We ask questions about them, too, mostly to answer questions about ourselves.

So where did you come from?

What are your beliefs about .....?

What music do you like?

We are just really asking another question about ourselves.

Is this person comparable with me?

Making another person the answer to your endless litany of questions about yourself is an unhealthy way of trying to find yourself in another person. I do not want to imply that asking questions is a bad thing, because it is not. But I think a simple shift in perspective can clear up quite a bit of confusion. Live with the other person being the question to which you are the answer. This requires listening, learning, and loving, and in the process of becoming the answer to their ever changing and endlessly challenging questions, you may discover who you really are in the process. Or at least be aware of who you really are becoming.

# Love Story
## ~ Traci

A suspended, undulating sphere
Trodden by guilty feet and fear.
Fractured ground, splintered souls
Desperate to uncover a pulse.

A suspended, undying Love
Our sins made Him a mourning dove.
Mending blood pours deep and wide
Sure to saturate His withering Bride.

Gently, He presses His ear to hear
Her chest rising and falling with fear.
"I am perfect Love. Open your lips and
see.
Breathe, Bride. Exhaling you, inhaling
Me."

His essence over her spirit glides
Penetrating until their hearts collide.
He reaches in and plucks hers out...
Replacing it with His own. "She is
Mine!" he shouts.

She shudders, eyes wide with rapture
Her chest rises, breathing deeply to
capture,
Heaven's heartbeat now within her,
eternally.
Intoxication, elation, joy and ecstasy.

"I have tasted. I have seen. What is this
passion?
It lies deep within. It is You. And me
You have fashioned.
Yet I cannot partake. Just look at me.
My garments, my clothes are tattered,
You see?"

"Brilliant Bride, I am unaware of what
you claim,
For My eyes see perfection and there is
no shame.
I gave you my robe. You are pure and
white as snow.
Every blemish, every stain...I no
longer know."

She sighs, desperate to believe His
words.

Afraid. She questions what she has just
heard.
"It's impossible. Once a prostitute, my
body marred,
Surely no mercy could be so strong.
Someday, You will discard."

He dives into her soul with His spheres
of grace,
Searching deeply within her, caressing
her face.
"It is finished. See My hands...there
you are engraved.
My blood has made you clean, no
longer enslaved.

Suddenly, an explosion in her soul!
Nearly convinced that she is whole...
Tempted to shrink back and pull away,
But He firmly draws her to Him. "I am
the Way."

"Open your lips. Breathe in deep.
My Bride. In My essence, you shall
sleep.
You will dream, then awaken and see

All that you are is all of Me."

Daring to open herself and bare her
soul,
She closes her eyes, her body falls into
His hold.
A surge of life vanquishes every doubt.
Living waters flow. The curtain falls
upon the drought.

A suspended, undulating sphere
Now carries the imprints of those that
are dear.
Purchased, embraced in His grace.
Forever before Him, beholding His
face.

# More Than the Stars

### ~ William

If you have ever been in love, you have likely been with that person outdoors at night. While feebly attempting to describe the enormity of the heart and passion for a person, countless individuals have looked at the glistening blackness of the stars overhead, and in a moment of delusional originality (because they think they are being original), they compare the scope of their love to the vastness of the cosmos and the cosmos loses on all counts.

Do you know how big the cosmos is? I mean, really. Have you ever been taught of the grandiose impossibility of attempting to describe the size of known space and the hundreds of billions of galaxies that are floating trillions of light years away? I did not think so, and it would not matter. You would still believe with irrational sincerity that your love for that person trumps in size, scope, and mystery, the vast wonders of the world within and beyond the known universe. And you would be right.

Love provokes us to make irrational claims that are absolutely true. God is love, and your profession of your hearts' overwhelming affection for someone gives you full access to compare your love to the scope of the heavens and say it is more than that for He is more than that. He is the fullness that fills all in all, and there is nowhere you can go where He cannot be found. So let the irrational claims flow, and be the voice of God, Who loves with a ferocity that makes the sun seem like just another ice cube in your glass of tea.

There is nothing illogical about giving language to a Truth that is beyond human comprehension: That you are loved by God and worth being

loved by one made in His image and
likeness.

# Laughter in the Darkness
## ~ Traci

I am beginning to believe that promise often comes with trial and terror. Throughout the Scriptures, there are many examples of God promising or revealing an extraordinary plan to His chosen ones, but before they arrive at the promise (and some miss the promise altogether due to their complaining), there is often trial, sorrow, and breaking. So it is with covenant.

As I read Genesis 15, I noticed some things about Abram and his experience with God as covenant was made between them. In verse 5, God shows Abram the trillions of twinkling stars in the sky and He promises Abram a seemingly impossible thing: an old man gaining a son of his own seed and having descendants as numerous as the stars! How laughable (hence, the name "Isaac"). Did

Abram's heart pump with excitement and joy? What an amazing promise!

Before Abram could break out the cocktails and plan a feast, God began to give Abram instructions, requesting various animals that would then be cut and laid out before the Lord. Abram laid each half of the animals opposite each other and then he waited. An interesting thing happened next. Verse 12: "Now when the sun was going down, a deep sleep fell upon Abram; and behold, terror and great darkness fell upon him." What? Terror in the midst of a covenant process with God?

Fear came after receiving a really cool promise from God? I do not get it. God then proceeds to give Abram a frightening word about the difficulty that would ensue. The Lord neatly packages the hair-raising word with a pretty little bow on top..."and afterward they will come out with many possessions. As for you, you shall go to your fathers in peace; you will be buried at a good old age." Sweet. Thanks for that.

What happened next really caught my attention: Genesis 15:17 says, "It came about when the sun had set, that it was very dark, and behold, there appeared a smoking oven and a flaming torch which passed between these pieces (of dead animals). Verse 18- On that day, the LORD made a covenant with Abram..."

I wonder why God waited until dark. Was it to enhance the stunning visual of a fire burning against the black sky? Or could it be that He likes to descend with His fire in the midst of our darkness? I vote for option number two.

So I pondered this thought for the rest of the day: It was in the midst of our darkness...it was while we were yet sinners...it was while we broke His heart...when we were well past fruit-bearing season, it was after sunset, when the atmosphere around us was black, that He came to make covenant with us.

He rejoices in bringing His light, His fire, His promise when we are sure that there is no hope of leaving a legacy. He comes with laughter..."Isaac". He makes a promise to us and lets us know that the road ahead may be rugged, rutted, and uneven, but His promise remains. His seed is in us and it is impossible for His seed to not bear something beautiful and full of life.

Remember, if you are awakened with terror and struggling with the pains of the course of your life, begin to laugh. He is about to intervene with a wondrous promise in the midst of your darkness. And when He does, lock it in your heart; never forgetting the goodness of God.

# Covenant

## ~ Traci

(As my husband and I were preparing to celebrate 19 years of marriage)

As our anniversary approaches, I feel a bittersweet joy, mixed with sorrow, when I ponder the number of our friends who have experienced the poison of loss...particularly the loss of covenant. I have watched many who are close to me wear the pain of betrayal on their faces; their bodies bear the death of a covenant. Smiles have weakened. Eyes that were once filled with joy, struggle to lift their lids long enough to dare to greet another day. Do they dare to love again?

God has brought covenant to my attention during this season. What is covenant, exactly? How durable is it, really? Can mankind ever keep a covenant and truly live a life of joy? I know there is a mystery regarding covenant that lies so deeply within the heart of God and it is something tangible, waiting to be discovered and experienced.

My husband has taught me, "Covenant always wins." More than anything, I want to believe that. And I think that I do. I know that God's covenant forever stands, and there is power in the blood of His beloved Son that maintains covenant that can never be destroyed. How can He not win?

As I have poured over many books of the Bible, like Hosea, Amos, Jeremiah, and many others, I see the pain in God's heart as He watches those He loves staggering in a cesspool of what they believe to be love. It is called deception. Yet, the Lover stands by, sometimes feeling the desire to destroy the very ones that He longed for in the beginning...yet His heart moves from anger to love, once again. He forgives. He continues to love. He woos. He gives. He even sets the perpetrators in positions of honor and uses them for His glory. Are we, as people, capable of that kind of love?

There have been moments when I feared loving. If you never want to hurt, then by all means, avoid relationship. However, in doing so, you forfeit the treasure of truly living...living deeply and living fully, and that would be the greatest pain of all. Living a life in which you never moved the heart of another, brought life to a soul, or allowed someone else to move your heart…that would be a tragedy. That is a pain that far outweighs the pain of loving.

Sometimes, the barrier to love is totally based on misperception, miscommunication and misunderstanding, which means that the barrier is based on lies. The barrier is merely an illusion. The only power that the enemy truly has is his lies. The lie holds no power until we choose to believe it, therefore, we are the ones who empower a lie and set it on course to bring destruction. Once a lie is believed, we have opened the door to the influence of darkness, and once we stick our foot in the door, we usually become convinced that there is no turning back, and that we might just stumble upon something we have longed for if we will continue justifying the lie.

A fog enters our mind, and slowly, sometimes suddenly, we are convinced that our mess is actually destiny. How deluded we become as we begin listening to the voice of hell itself. Stolen destinies are often born out of pausing at the barrier to love just long enough to take a glance, thinking perhaps that what we once thought was love may have actually been a farce, so we move into a trap, believing we will be set free.

So, what of misperception? What of miscommunication? Sometimes a lack of communication is the culprit. In my case, my husband and I recently uncovered a slightly hilarious misperception in our own relationship. After almost 19 years of marriage, we discovered that my face was the problem. I have a weak muscle on the left side of my face that causes my closed-lip smile to appear as a smirk, when viewed from the left. Since my husband is often the one who drives our vehicle while we are on the road, he could only see the left side of my face, seemingly smirking, after he would unfold a joke or brilliant thought.

All along, I was amused, enjoying his thoughts, but from the appearance of my face, he interpreted my look as the presence of contempt, viewing him as a fool who lacked the ability to capture my heart with his communication. Talk about sad. Thank God we discovered what was really happening! Now we can enjoy conversation and he knows that I am not putting him down with my visage. Learn the face of your lover.

I once had a dream where Jesus took me to Heaven, to a special room that contained a magnificent, blue stone that sent a blanket of blue light that covered the earth. He looked at me and said, "This is My Hope Diamond." I later realized that our sky is blue because it reflects His hope for all of creation. God literally envelops us, His entire creation, in His hope. He never gives up on us. This revelation helped me to understand why when battling disappointment, nighttime seems to be the most difficult. The black night sky conceals the reflection of His hope for His creation.

I am reminded of various places in

the Bible that mention looking up. "I lift up mine eyes…" "Lift up your heads…" I once heard that if you lift up your head or look up while thinking a negative thought, the thought loses its power to depress you more deeply. When looking down, the depression quickly sets in and is intensified. Is that not amazing? The next time you are feeling down, look up and gaze into the blue sky. Gaze upon the hope that He has for you.

Back to marriage and covenant: Is there anything interfering with your marriage covenant? Is there anything you dare not tell your spouse? If so, lay it all out on the table and cut off the ties that are interfering with true intimacy. A safe place is truly a safe place when there is total honesty within covenant. A secret sin unconfessed becomes a stronghold. You are only as sick as your secrets. The enemy has a way of making that "secret place" feel safe, when in reality, the only safe place is in God's secret place, where hearts are exposed and covenant is restored and celebrated.

Have you ever thought about how the enemy tries to interfere with God's covenant with you? It is only through lies. By getting you to believe lies, he can cause you to lose the intense enjoyment of the covenant that has been promised to you. In the natural, this is what is reflected in marriages. Where there is division and turmoil, there is a lie at the core that someone is believing and acting upon. When we believe a lie, we are putting our faith in the lie. And faith is a powerful force.

(Before I continue, in the following paragraphs, I am not speaking about abusive situations). The grass is NOT greener on the other side. I have known some Christians to attempt to justify affairs and unnecessary divorce, saying that their marriage was not

God's will. As if God said to them, "Oops. I meant this one! That marriage served its purpose. Now, come try this out." No! However, He does have a way of bringing beautiful things out of our crappy situations.

If you are lacking pleasure and connection in your marriage, it is only an invitation to seek it within your spouse and find the treasure that lies within. If you are too exhausted for the adventure of rediscovery, my prayer for you is that you are supernaturally recharged and reignited in passion for your spouse. Honestly, some of the deepest discoveries and rediscoveries are birthed in some of the most painful circumstances. Never give up. This is where faith is tested and proven to be effective.

I am asking God for new revelation on covenant. I believe that there is such a deep mystery about covenant that remains to be unfolded, and I want to see it, because I am thirsting and hungering for the key to true, lasting, loving, beautiful, fulfilling covenant. I do not want to witness the look of overwhelming pain in the faces of those that I love. Jesus paid a heavy, painful price and I want Him to get what He paid for. He paid for us. He paid for covenant. He paid a price for you to have a fulfilling marriage. He deserves everything and everyone that He bled for.

# Discerning in the Dark
## ~ William

There are so many people I know
that have this cloud of despair over
their eyes that hinders their ability to
see the goodness of God in their lives.
Ok, I hate it, too, when some preacher
starts telling you about all these people
who have issues as if he is going to tell
you how he fixed them and can fix
you, too.

The truth is that I could not write
about the cloud if I had not crawled
around in it myself a few times. When
you are a minister, though it makes
you empathetic on the inside, you just
look pathetic on the outside. I strongly
dislike seeing people in a helpless
despair. Watching people close to you
walk out such torment is a kind of
torment in itself.

We know that the answer lies in the
power of the Holy Spirit. But to say to
a depressed person that all he or she

has to do is lay hold of that would be like telling me that all I have to do to get healthier is to bench press 300 pounds ten times a day. The advice is true but physically I am not in a place where I can accomplish that. People who are facing depression are not in a place where they have the will to lay hold of the answer on their own. But what if the Answer lays hold of you?

The power of prayer is in the power of agreement and many people are not in a place mentally to come into agreement with the Word of God. Offense toward God is a cancer in the soul. The lens of bitterness can literally make the Scripture look like it means what it does not and can cause every word that is spoken that can bring life to become twisted where, in the mind of one in depression, it brings death. You may have come to a place where you have bought into an unholy agreement and empowered it through unforgiveness.

Before you realize what is going on, you believe the lies that say you have failed, that you have missed it (the plan and purpose of God), that you cannot face another day, that life is an enemy to you, that death is a friend, that others would be better off without you, that God has turned a blind eye toward your self destruction, and that everything is just too hard. Satan will do to you the same thing he did to Adam and Eve. He will talk and talk until you agree or rebuke him.

There are areas of my life where I have gone off course, and in every instance I can trace it back to two things that became an unspoken reality in my heart. I developed an offense at God, and I carried internal guilt and shame. So today I invite you to make a conscious and purposeful declaration with me from your heart. "I will never blame God, and I will never allow guilt and shame to infect me." God is good, and Christ is for you.

## The Power of a Kiss
## ~ Traci

And the Lord God formed man of the dust of the ground, and breathed into his nostrils the breath of life; and man became a living soul. (Genesis 2:7)

In the beginning, when the earth was without form, and void, the Creator simply spoke things into being. "Let there be light." "Let there be…" But when it came to man, He took the time to lovingly dip His hands into the dust that He had made. He crafted an intricate sculpture, inside and out, shaping and molding every muscle and bone. He could have said, "Let there be man" or "Let him come to life," but instead, He placed His mouth over Adam's lifeless face and breathed His very own breath into him. Imagine the heart beginning to pump. Blood, the life-force surging through his veins. Adam's very first breath was a gift from the Father. The kiss of life.

In John 20:19, Jesus breathed on His disciples the breath of life that would infuse them with His heartbeat, filling them with His Spirit, to be carriers and distributors of life. The kiss of life, once again. Man fully restored to his original intent.

Every time I think about the power of breath, life, and the kiss, I cannot wait to press my lips to my husbands' lips. I feel life surge through my veins. There is an exchange of life that takes place, and if you pay attention, you too will feel the power of that exchange. Be conscious of the life of God within you. Breathe into your spouse the breath of Heaven. You will feel something you have never felt before. If you are having problems communicating or even with loving your spouse, pray and ask God to infuse you with His presence and then lay your lips on your spouse and

release life. If at first you don't
succeed, try, and try again.

# Home is a Person
## ~ William

I have always felt like a homeless nomad. There are a couple of perspectives you develop when you grow up in a house on wheels. One is where you really do not feel like you belong anywhere and cannot seem to find your place. The other is when you make peace with that existence to the point where everywhere feels like home. I have seen it both ways, often at the same time, which was really confusing when I was six years old.

I grew up in a missionary/evangelist house where we were always moving. To find reason to get out of the trailer and slap it a couple of times and send it on its way was a temptation at a few places from the mountains of Estes Park Colorado to the beaches of Clearwater, Florida. But it was not a place where I found home. It was a person. Traci had barely been out of the Austin city limits.  She fell in love with a traveler and I fell in love with a deeply rooted "Yellow Rose of Texas."  We agreed to meet in the middle and have found home in one another most of the time and almost everywhere ever since. I think falling in love with someone is like finding your way home.  And it is that nomadic hunger for home that leads many to Jesus Christ.

After all of the books, sermons, movies, and even the words of Christ Himself, Jesus is still an uncharted land whose borders have yet to be defined. The unflinching honesty, mercy, compassion, vengeance, and wisdom left him an unpredictable mystery to the point that even when He told His disciples what He would do, they were still surprised when it actually happened. At His departure He promised that His Spirit would guide disciples in their lives from then on, providing the needed peace to those rare individuals who would take up that offer and in doing so, follow the unpredictable whims of God as His love and glory cover the earth like water.

If one claims to be a follower of Jesus Christ, you would best keep your shoes tied and your hands open. Be ready to move and hold onto nothing. Nothing but Christ. When one holds fast to Christ, the ability to enjoy life is amplified. We desire to possess but we often fail to enjoy that which we fight to possess. In Christ, we may possess little, but enjoy much. In this abundance of life we find hope.

The fact that the collective mass of society rejects this hope is reflected in the church's methodology of marketing the Gospel to get the attention of that collective mass by any means necessary. Yet God sought to hide this eternal treasure in the simplicity of this mysterious, homeless individual who could calm a churning sea with a word and make blind eyes see with spit and mud. What do you do with a man like that? Apparently, you kill him. But only if you do not realize that He is your home.

# God's Cry
## ~ Traci

As I fell asleep this afternoon, I began to dream of the world. I could see people all over the earth and I heard the voice of God, crying, "Will you make a place for Me inside of your heart...a place for Me to hold onto, where I can pull Myself into You? When I come in, our hearts will be one. You in Me. I in You. You will know My voice. We will speak as one."

Then I saw husbands and wives stepping into each other, their hearts melting into one. When this happened, there was amazing power that went out. The only way I know to describe it is a love-light...the goodness of God...the love of Jesus that shined out from each "unit" (couple) and the world was filled with joy.

I thought about how marriage is a

picture of God's relationship with us, His Bride...how He longs for us, and how powerful it is when we desire Him so much that we surrender to His heart. Can you imagine what the world would look like if each of us surrendered to God 100%, body, soul, mind and spirit? Can you imagine what the world would look like if every husband and wife fell in love with each other again, totally surrendering their hearts to each other? He in us. Us flooding the earth with His goodness.

Jesus surrendered His heart to us when He died on the cross. All we have to do is surrender our hearts to Him. Simple exchange. Bountiful results.

# Savior Love
## ~ Traci

Love-drenched pools of
compassionate tenderness. Hazel
jewels that grant pardon to the
weakest. A menial soul held captive,
lost in the expanse of a sea so dark; the
unexpecting heart at first refrains from
the touch of the liberating salvager,
finally giving in to the emancipating
kiss. Unchained. Unbound. Discharged
from the watery grave where it was
found.

"Do you see what I see?" Love

asks.

Love stands.

A response seems to have such little

meaning, for there are no adequate

words to express this newfound rush of

life, essence and vitality...too deep to

speak its interpretation. What action,

what touch, what verbalization exists to do justice to the love of One who spilled His blood?

Love-drenched, hazel pools that grant pardon to the weakest and the lowest. When shame attempts its wicked hold on the chosen vessels, Love breathes long and deep, piercing the clay with its magnificent river, moving debris far away...free to fall. In. Love. Falling into Him.

And above all things have fervent love for one another, for "love will cover a multitude of sins."

1 Peter 4:8

## Real Love?
## ~ Traci

I once thought that I loved as
deeply as a human could possibly love,
but as time goes on, I realize that I
may not know the first thing about real
love. Maybe I just loved the best that I
knew how, and God smiled at that as a
father smiles at his child who just
learned how to stand. The child may
feel proud that he can stand, yet there
are so many things yet to accomplish,
like walking, running, jumping,
hopping on one foot, leaping,
climbing, swimming, mastering skills,
and so on.

Perhaps the level of love that I
knew was just the beginning...the baby
steps. The challenge in learning to love
like Jesus is that there is pain involved
and sometimes there is pain that goes
so deep, you can barely breathe, let
alone stand. Moving from the
beginning of love into its deepest

depths requires a stretching, tearing, and moving of the heart that leaves us in awe of our ability to survive it.

Is it possible to love so deeply and freely that the pain of disappointment and loss cannot shake your heart and soul? Is it possible to continue loving, without fear, even though you know that disappointment is right around the corner?

I have always believed that love is a choice. You can choose to love. I still believe that to some extent, but there is a love that goes deeper and it is simply a gift. A friend told me that if one has to try to trust, then there IS no trust. If one has to try to love, then something is lacking. Perhaps, maybe taking the action can create a reality, but I would rather that God flood me with the gift of love and trust.

Christians often pray for boldness. I have prayed for boldness many times, but now I realize that all I need is love. If I am overflowing with the love of God, I will not need boldness. Boldness without love can be cruel and obnoxious. But love is the passion that drives us to do the impossible.

My parents have a recording of me as a child, reading the verse: "Perfect love casts out fear." I suppose that God knew I would need to hear that verse, in my own voice, reciting to my own ears the truth that would bring me freedom in the future. I thought, "What is perfect love?" The answer is Jesus. He is perfect love, so if I am full of His Spirit, I will walk in perfect love. This is my prayer today: "Jesus, fill me with Yourself, that I will become love personified; a mighty, overflowing river of life and peace that touches everyone and everything in its path. This is what I desire to be. A river of love." What is your prayer?

# All Things New
## ~ Traci

Floodgates
Dams
Deep calls to deep
Barriers
Walls
Safer to let the heart sleep
Cracking
Opening
From it, sorrows seep
Flowing
Weaving
Ancient wounds leap
Over
Under
Around
Beyond
Hurting places hidden in song
A melody formed
To encapsulate pain
Shofar blows
Trumpet cries
Breaking blinders from our eyes
New

Restored
Breathing again
For real
Life
Peace
Rivers of joy
Gladness
Smiles
A diamond is birthed
Pleasures unearthed
Tears of love
Bittersweet love
Capturing joy in the dust
Settling
Smoothing
Waking the heart
This love is real
Hands
Eyes
Lips
That release
A Savior's heart
To every beast
Peace
Shalom
Be still

And know
You are not alone
He is God
Faithful
Promising
All things new

## To Curse or Not to Curse
## ~ Traci

Who are we to curse a city or region? We are priests and kings on this earth. What kind of king would destroy the very kingdom that was handed down to him through the painful, sacrificial death of his father?

Jesus paid a heavy price and He gave us authority and the responsibility to take cities under our wings…under His wings, because God said that He wills that none should perish. So we should will the same.

We are called to look into a dark city and find the gold within. To see her destiny and wrap our arms around her people and bring them into the fold, where they belong. Genesis 1 tells us that the Spirit of God hovered over the darkness, the formless void that was earth. He hovered, laid Himself over the emptiness and breathed the words, "Let there be light," and there was light.

In our cities, there are empty vessels that bear a void so deep and dark; and they pant for the water of life. These vessels were created for the glory of God. They were meant to be His.

Upon entering a region, let us declare that His Spirit is hovering over them and let us come into agreement with the words of our Father and say, "Let there be light." It is our duty because God's prized creation lives there. When God created the world, He spoke everything into being, but when it came to man, He used His hands to form and create. He lovingly breathed into man, giving His own breath to make us living souls. He did not impart breath and life to man only to have man and his heirs be destroyed. No! Humanity is destined to live and thrive, free from the chains of darkness.

When we look into the darkness of cities and various regions, as priests and kings, we are commanded to look and recognize the Father's breath in its vessels and say, "That's it! That is my Father's breath that gives them life and makes them move. Those are the veins yet to know His blood." Jesus wants His Bride to lay her head on His chest, to hear His heartbeat and know His voice. He desires that everyone come into His heart, into the safe place.

Jesus is the Word (John 1:1) and He is one with God, the Father, and Holy Spirit. When the Father breathed into Adam, He filled mankind with the Word. His Word does not return void.

For man to perish is like God's Word returning void…and that should never be. His words bring life and so do ours. Choose life, not death. Choose blessing, not cursing. Be the breath of life to someone else and remember that when we speak against other believers, we are attacking Jesus' Bride and Body. Be a king, and save a city.

## Being Born Again
## ~ Traci

What does it mean to be born again? I ponder….

Before birth, we breathe amniotic fluid, the life-sustaining substance of the womb that envelops us and protects us. We are fed and given life by the connection to our mothers' blood supply. Being born again places us in the "womb" of Heaven where we breathe in the liquid love of God. We drown in the essence of our Creator, yet it is a drowning that brings life, never death.

We thrive on our connection to His Spirit. The heartbeat of God feeds us, nourishes us, and grows us. When we learn to be in that place, we can step into the world and live and breathe, cord never cut. In Him we live and move and have our being. We can live the life we were created for, in communion with the One who first loved us.

Being born again requires the dying of the old (ways and identities), laying down our flesh and all that is attached to it…drowning willingly so that we may live. Birth can be violent, yet there is rest and peace, awe and wonder waiting to be seen.

Do You Know That I Love You?
~ Traci

"I love you."

What do I mean when I say it?

Rather, shall I ask, "Do you know that I love you?"

Will I fear the response?

Before I breathe the words, "I love you," I must ask myself, "Have I been patient? Have I been kind? Have I envied? Have I paraded myself? Been puffed up? Have I behaved rudely? Have I sought my own way? Have I been easily provoked? Have I thought evil? Have I rejoiced in iniquity? Do I rejoice in truth? Do I bear all things, believe all things, hope all things and endure all things?"

# Unshackled

## ~ Traci

Winter woods

Fettered Trees

Covered in winters' darkness

Broken branches

Fallen leaves


Resurrected woods

Unshackled trees

Saturated in Love's righteousness

Mended branches

Restored leaves


Forever revived

True Love's kiss

Beloved Bride

Eternally His

For the Father judges no one, but has committed all judgment to the Son…

~ John 5:22

# A Word from Britain Vanderbush

Why do we fear love? Because we fear having to give something in return. We fear someone saying they love us and not being able to genuinely respond the way that they want us to. We fear others saying that they love us because we fear that we do not have the time, the strength, or the capacity within our hearts to return the love that we are given. Yet each one of us desires a love so deep and impenetrable that death itself could not take it from our grasp. We are caught in this plane, this dimension in life in which we wait for a love that could already be very much alive within our hearts.

What if, for one day, you did not fear love? What if you accepted it freely and let it envelop you and become you? What if you realized that you could love each person you meet so deeply that you needed nothing in return? And what if that love is the thing that saves their lives? What if it could save yours?

This flesh and these bones, they are not us. They are natural substances of the earth, and we are but the spirits who get to control and inhabit them for the moment. Outside of this mortal body and beyond this plane of existence, we could be endless and boundless, stretching beyond galaxies, living outside of time and space. If so, then how much further stretches our love? And if not, how capable of great love are we still? If God is love and we are made in His image and likeness, would that not also make us... Love? So then it must be true that to love another is to see the face of God. It must be true that when we are truly filled with love, our spirit must resonate in a wonderful way with His.

So why can I not look at you and say, "You owe me nothing. You need to do nothing other than be yourself to deserve it... You do not have to do anything to maintain it. You do not have to fear it. It simply is something that is. And it is something that cannot be taken away... I love you?"

One soul to another, one heart to another, why do we fear the love that comes from one another? For the same reason we fear the love that comes from God. We think it demands something of us. When truly, it demands nothing. Love's intent... is to love. You are loved.

**YOU ARE LOVED
OUTRAGEOUSLY.**

14665829R00101